Happiness Now!

By Bruce Mulkey

7.14.13

To Elaine Alpert

Thank you so much for bringing your full self to this weekend and sharing your wisdom and skills with us in an extraordinary way.
With love and respect,
Bruce

Happiness Now!

Copyright © 2011 by Bruce Mulkey, Asheville, North Carolina, USA

All rights reserved. No part of this book may be used or reproduced in any manner without the written permission of the author.

Editor: Susan Snowden, Snowden Editorial Services

Cover art and design: David Lynch, Lynch Graphics

Cover photograph: Shonnie Lavender

Title inspiration: Frank Costanza, "The Serenity Now," *Seinfeld*

ISBN 978-1-257-76927-8

Printed in the United States of America

Published by Lulu Press

June 2011

Table of Contents

Introduction viii

SIMPLY BEING HAPPY 1

Choose happiness 2

Make happiness a habit...3

Smile your way to happiness 4

Laughter is the best medicine 5

Take action to be happy 6

Nurture yourself regularly 7

Remember to breathe deeply 8

Spend time in nature 9

Take time for "being" 10

Simplify your life..11

Make your home a sanctuary 12

Care for your physical health 13

DEEPENING YOUR HAPPINESS 15

Tell the truth..16

Keep your word 17

Express your love 18

Acknowledge others...19

Express your gratitude 20

Refuse to be judgmental 21
Steer clear of gossip 22
Forgive for your own good 23
Use affirming language 24
Be conscious of what you ingest 25
Choose what enters your awareness 26
Take time to play 27
Handle your addictions 28
Engage in a spiritual practice 29
Take time for solitude 30
Find a mentor 31

HAPPINESS AND AUTHENTICITY 33
Become fully accountable 34
Resign as emperor of the universe 35
Notice the messages life sends 36
Live authentically 37
Live your deepest values 38
Reclaim your integrity 39
Live in the moment 40
Tame your inner critic 41
Dispose of limiting beliefs 42
Handle disconnections as you go 43

Bless your past and let it go 44
Stretch yourself regularly 45
Create meaningful rituals 46
Do your best in all you do 47
Dwell in a locale that fits 48

HAPPINESS IN RELATIONSHIPS 49

Love and nurture yourself 50
Surround yourself with supporters 51
Create a loving relationship 52
Deepen all your relationships 53
Treat your children well 54
More hugs = more happiness 55
Fully commit 56
Hear and be heard 57
Ask for what you want 58
Clearly state "yes" or "no" 59
Don't take it personally 60
Establish boundaries 61
Create a support network 62

HAPPINESS . . . TO JOY 63
- Create a vision for yourself 64
- Live your purpose 65
- Harness the power of intention 66
- Appreciate the web of life 67
- Share your gifts through service 68
- Keep on keeping on 69

HAPPY ENDINGS 71
- Make friends with death 72
- Things to do before you die 73
- About the author 74

Dedicated to the happiest person I know . . .
my daughter Gracelyn Lavender Mulkey,
whose photograph graces the cover of this book.

Happiness is the meaning and the purpose of life, the whole aim and end of human existence.

~Aristotle

Introduction

You can be happy if you want to be. While you may have little control over the events around you, you have total control of the happiness in your own life.

Each of us has a level of happiness (or unhappiness) to which we've become accustomed. Yet you can move to a higher level: You simply resolve to make conscious choices for yourself that will increase your happiness level, and you take action on a regular basis until you create and adapt to a more joyful way of life.

In this little book I have made a number of suggestions for raising one's level of happiness. I created these suggestions for you . . . and for me, since many of them are lessons I want in my consciousness, or in some cases to relearn after having forgotten them . . . again.

I acknowledge you for your willingness to begin this journey and take ownership of the quality of your life. If not now, when?

SIMPLY BEING HAPPY

*Just get out of the business of
fixing yourself and attempting
to fix all the others,
and get into the business,
that delightful business,
of simply being happy.*

~Roy Whitten, *Simply Being Happy*

*There's nothing you have to do.
You want to be happy? Be happy.*

~Neale Donald Walsch

Choose happiness

Your happiness is not dependent on what's happening out there; it depends on what's happening inside you. It's not a matter of chance; it's a matter of choice. Whenever you really choose to do so, you can be happy. How about right now?

Most folks are about as happy as they make up their minds to be.

~Abraham Lincoln

Make happiness a habit

How do you make happiness a habit? Start with breathing deeply, relaxing your body, lightening up, perhaps even smiling. Create a happiness mantra: "I choose happiness." "I look on the bright side of life." "I am a happy person." Use whatever words work for you. And when you find your state of happiness slipping away, breathe, relax, smile, and repeat your mantra as many times as you need to to shift back to happiness.

In following this practice, you begin to reset your happiness level, and you make happiness your natural state of being.

Sometimes your joy is the source of your smile, but sometimes your smile can be the source of your joy.

~Thich Nhat Hanh

Smile your way to happiness

Research indicates that when you smile you stimulate an unconscious response in your brain, and you actually begin to feel happier. So even when you're not really feeling happy, you can move in that direction by simply choosing to smile.

What do you think would happen if you broke into a big grin right now?

Laughter is the sensation of feeling good all over and showing it principally in one place.

~Josh Billings

Laughter is the best medicine

Laughter is a great indicator that we're truly feeling happy. It's well known that laughter provides great benefits to body, mind, and spirit. In fact, there are folks who have recovered from disease, depression, and other ailments merely with large doses of merriment and glee.

As children we laughed often and exuberantly. As adults, we typically tone down our frivolity. But there are lots of opportunities for hilarity and fun—humorous companions, amusing books, light-hearted movies, hilarious TV shows, mirthful cartoons, entertaining comedy clubs, side-splitting jokes, and much more.

What really tickles your funny bone? When do you find yourself laughing out loud? How about making a cheerful choice for yourself today?

Fill what's empty, empty what's full, and scratch where it itches.

~The Duchess of Windsor

Take action to be happy

What activities, people, situations, environments, et cetera, help create a feeling of happiness for you? Perhaps it's an inspiring movie. Perhaps it's a deep conversation with a good friend. Perhaps it's a solitary walk in the woods. The possibilities are, of course, limitless.

To help you get started, complete this sentence: I feel happy when I . . . Do this several times. Then choose at least one action from this exercise and do it.

There's no better way to energize your body, mind, and spirit than by taking care of yourself.

~Stephanie Tourles

Nurture yourself regularly

If you want to really be happy, take care of your deepest wants and needs on an ongoing basis. Get that massage, take a nap, go for a long walk, prepare a tasty and nutritious meal for yourself, read your favorite book, meditate, spend time at your spiritual practice.

When you treat yourself in this manner, you not only get the immediate results—say from the massage—you also get a profound inner sense that you value yourself. Self-respect grows, and self-esteem is engendered. This will lead to gifting yourself with more self-nurturing, thus greater self-respect and self-esteem, in a continuous loop that propels you toward greater happiness.

What is one thing you will do to nurture yourself today?

Emotional and physical states can be altered by changing the breathing pattern.

~Wilhelm Reich

Remember to breathe deeply

When you breathe naturally and deeply, you release stress, tension, and even anxiety, thereby creating room for happiness to take root.

Many of us typically engage in shallow breathing, using only a portion of our lungs to take in the life-giving oxygen we need. Learn to breathe more deeply: Take a class on the subject, read a book, research it on the internet. You'll not only be happier, you'll become more energetic, more focused, more centered, and healthier.

Right now . . . take eight slow, deep breaths; relax and enjoy the results.

The best remedy for those who are afraid, lonely or unhappy is to go outside. . . . Because only then does one feel that all is as it should be and that God wishes to see people happy, amidst the simple beauty of nature.

~Anne Frank

Spend time in nature

Many of us spend very little time in the natural world and, thus, suffer from what some call nature deficit disorder. We tend to move from one human-made structure to another, from one air-conditioned space to the next. This is a radical departure from the way humans lived for tens of thousands of years, and it's not without consequences.

We need our time in nature to feel the rhythms of the seasons, release the overly domesticated part of ourselves and remember who we really are. We need to be among the wildlife to remind us that we too are animals with our place in the web of life. We need time in the natural world to reawaken our sense of wonder and awe.

To raise your happiness level, spend at least a few minutes outdoors each day, and, if possible, go into the wilderness for a few hours during the week to commune quietly with nature.

Doing is a function of the body. Being is a function of the soul. The body is always doing something. . . . It is a state of beingness the soul is after, not a state of doingness.

~Neale Donald Walsch

Take time for "being"

Many of us base our self-worth, and thus our happiness, on getting our tasks done. Our culture certainly promotes this perspective, and who are we to go against the grain? Instead of focusing on your to-do list, how about taking some time to relax and just be?

For a few moments, let go of what you "should" be doing, let your breathing slow, let your gaze soften, let your body relax, let go of the chatter in your mind, and quietly "be."

Simplicity is the essence of happiness.
~Cedric Bledsoe

Simplify your life

Our culture invites us to overload ourselves with work obligations, social functions, volunteer activities, shopping, housekeeping, even recreational activities. Many of us are so busy that we rarely take time to relax and recall why we're here and what we want to do with our lives.

Being fully engaged—at work, at home, in the community—is important. But if we want to be happy, it's also important to know when to say no. So consciously choose what activities really fit for you and let the rest go.

You might also consider reducing the clutter in your home by getting rid of the superfluous and buying fewer new things. After all, will possessing that shiny new gizmo actually make you happier? If so, for how long?

Consider this: what can you do right now to simplify your life and create greater happiness?

A house is not a home unless it contains food and fire for the mind as well as the body.

~Margaret Fuller

Make your home a sanctuary

We all need a safe haven—a place of respite, a place that nourishes us, a place where we feel happy.

You can create your home as such a sanctuary. First handle all the disarray and all the things that need repair. If you have more "stuff" than comfortably fits in your home, sell, give away, or throw some of it out. If the towel rack in your bathroom is loose, fix it or replace it. If the carpet is dirty, get it cleaned.

Then decorate your home in a manner that reflects who you really are, in colors you love, in a way that fills you with joy and peaceful energy when you enter. Next, surround yourself with mementoes that reflect your true self—pictures of your successes, photos of loved ones and mentors, clippings that represent how you want to be or what you hope to achieve.

When you're finished, sit back, take it all in, and let the satisfaction and joy wash over you.

If you have health, you probably will be happy, and if you have health and happiness, you have all the wealth you need, even if it is not all you want.

~Elbert Hubbard

Care for your physical health

It's a lot easier to be happy when you're in good physical health. So here's the deal:

- Eat lots of tasty fruits, vegetables, and whole grains, preferably organic.
- Drink plenty of filtered water, and keep your intake of soft drinks and caffeinated beverages to a minimum.
- Choose exercise that's fun and that often includes other people.
- Determine how much sleep you need to be at your best, and get it.
- Deal with all physical health issues promptly and effectively.

Besides the anticipated benefits of excellent physical health, caring for yourself in this manner will engender a deeper sense of happiness and well-being within you.

DEEPENING YOUR HAPPINESS

When all your desires are distilled
You will cast just two votes:
To love more,
And be happy.

~Hafiz

No one can be happy who has been thrust outside the pale of truth. And there are two ways that one can be removed from this realm: by lying, or by being lied to.

~Lucius Annaeus Seneca

Tell the truth

Resolve to tell the plain, unvarnished truth at all times. When you eliminate white lies, half-truths, avoidance, omissions, withholding, and every other form of falsehood, you move toward reclaiming your integrity, your wholeness, your happiness. You don't have to struggle to create believable fictions. You eliminate the anxiety of trying to remember what you told to whom. There is no hesitation, no phoniness, no pretense.

When offering someone a truth that may be hard to hear, do so with caring and compassion. However, if someone reacts to your truth by feeling hurt, remember that that's their reaction for which they are responsible. You may wish to offer your love and support in such a situation, but it's not necessary to get hooked into accepting the blame for any distress they may be feeling.

Make your word law! . . . If you say it, live up to it lovingly.

~Wayne Dyer

Keep your word

It's simple: for a higher level of happiness, when you say you'll do something, do it. Period.

By taking on this discipline, you will likely become more conscious of what you commit to and what you decline. Keeping your word will help you get clear on when you really want to do something and when you don't. Furthermore, a solid no is easier for others to hear than a wishy-washy maybe or a half-hearted yes any day.

Finally, don't neglect to keep the commitments you make to yourself. When you tell yourself you're going to lay off the chocolate cake or you're going to be in bed by 10:30, keep your word.

Honoring your word to yourself and others is an essential part of keeping your integrity intact and your happiness high.

The key to happiness is to decide for love—consciously, willingly, and now!

~Marianne Williamson

Express your love

To be happy, give your love away freely. There's plenty more where it came from. Express it toward those closest to you—in words and in deeds. Send loving thoughts into the world—to those you know and those you don't know. Give your love to fellow humans, to the other animals of the world, to all living things, to the earth itself.

When you do so, you are not only nurturing others; you are nurturing yourself . . . by the selfless act of loving and through your connection with every living thing on this planet. For what you do for another, you also do for yourself.

The power of positive praise is limited only by its lack of use. . . . Silent appreciation doesn't mean much. Let others know you value them. They'll live up to your expectations.

~Glenn Van Ekeren

Acknowledge others

It's easy to acknowledge someone who wins the big prize, scores the winning touchdown, or gets married. But what about the person who opens the door for us, the coworker who volunteers to help, the mate who draws a warm bath for us at the end of a long day?

You can't say "thank you" too many times. You can't say "I really appreciate your thoughtfulness" too often. You can't say "I love you just because you're you" too frequently.

Look for ways to acknowledge the people around you—for what they've done and how they've been, for the big things and the little ones. Catch folks doing something good, and acknowledge them for it. Catch yourself doing something good, and acknowledge yourself for it too. You'll be happier, and those around you will be too.

Gratefulness is the key to a happy life that we hold in our hands, because if we are not grateful, then no matter how much we have we will not be happy—because we will always want to have something else or something more.

~David Steindl-Rast

Express your gratitude

To be truly happy, it's important to take a few moments each day to recall the things for which you're grateful. Perhaps you're grateful for successfully completing a project at work. Perhaps you're grateful for the loving smile of your mate. Perhaps you're grateful for this precious life you've been given.

You might consider creating a daily ritual during which you take a few moments to express your gratitude. One possibility: at the end of each day make a list of some of the people, events, and activities for which you're thankful.

By expressing your sincere gratitude, you're more aware of the gifts you've been given, and your happiness level is sure to rise.

*If you judge people,
you have no time to love them.*

~Mother Teresa

Refuse to be judgmental

When are your judgments of others most likely to arise? When you see someone smoking? When you are confronted with a parent being harsh with a child? When politicians appear to be misusing their power for their own gain?

In truth, your judgments are most likely to crop up when you are judging yourself. Thus your judgment of others is merely your outward projection of the traits or qualities you deem unacceptable in yourself.

How likely are you to be happy when you're judging yourself in this manner? Why not give up being the judge, jury, and executioner . . . of yourself as well as others?

It is one of my sources of happiness never to desire a knowledge of other people's business.

~Dolley Madison

Steer clear of gossip

Gossip is malicious chatter about the private affairs of others. Such scandal mongering is designed to make those who indulge in it feel better about themselves at the expense of others. It may seem to work in the short term, but eventually such unloving, disrespectful behavior results in "dis-ease" and disconnection for those who engage in it.

Remember that whoever gossips to you will also gossip about you. Any time a friend or acquaintance starts a sentence with "Did you hear about . . . ?" you can almost be assured that gossip is about to follow.

To raise your happiness level, refuse to engage in gossip or be with those who do.

To forgive is the highest, most beautiful form of love. In return, you will receive untold peace and happiness.

~Robert Muller

Forgive for your own good

It's impossible to really be happy while holding onto resentment. Resentment is a poison that pollutes your body, mind, and spirit. It not only disconnects you from the person toward whom you are resentful; resentment toward anyone blocks you from connecting as deeply with your closest loved ones. And it prevents you from connecting with that best part of yourself.

Refusing to hold ill will against another is just good sense. For who is suffering from the resentment you hold? It's not the intended recipient; it's you! As long as you hold ill will toward the "perpetrator," you are playing the victim, making your happiness contingent on what someone else did or did not do. Take back your power by forgiving—for good.

By forgiving—yourself and others—you feel a profound lightness, a deep sense of relief, and a greater sense of personal authority. Having cleaned out this malevolent emotional baggage, you have made more room for truly being happy.

Often it is the words we ourselves choose that have the greatest influence in our lives—affecting how we feel emotionally, function physically, and relate to others.

~Shonnie Lavender

Use affirming language

When you use affirming language, you create greater self-confidence, self-esteem, and happiness in your life. Some examples:

- **State what you want rather than what you don't want.** Change "I don't want to be late" to "I want to arrive on time."
- **Eliminate "I should," "I ought to," "I have to," and "I must."** Substitute "I will" or "I choose to" instead.
- **Stop "trying" and just do it.** Besides, you really can't try to do something; you do it or you don't.
- **Do away with "good" and "bad."** "Good" and "bad" are words we often use to judge ourselves and others. You might replace these words with "I want" or "I prefer."
- **Watch out for "yes, but . . ."** Using this phrase has the effect of erasing whatever came before it.

Start using more affirming language today, and increase the level of your happiness!

Take care of yourself. Good health is everyone's major source of wealth. Without it, happiness is almost impossible.

~Unknown

Be conscious of what you ingest

Imagine that you've received a gift from a wealthy uncle—one of the most superb automobiles made, a new Lamborghini. Imagine how you would treat this prized car so that it would function at its peak capacity for years to come, perhaps even a lifetime.

Well, you have been given a gift, perhaps the finest ever created—your human body. And this gift is definitely intended to last a lifetime. So how will you treat this body? Will you pollute it with junk food and sweets? Or will you choose fruits, vegetables, and grains free from additives and pesticides? Will you contaminate it with sugar-laden soft drinks, caffeinated beverages, and alcohol? Or will you keep it well hydrated with pure water and fresh juice? Will you defile it with drugs and tobacco? Or will you abstain from such harmful substances?

Begin creating a higher level of happiness in your life today by consciously choosing what you'll put in the precious body you've been given.

*You must weed your mind as
you would weed your garden.*

~Astrid Alaudat

Choose what enters your awareness

You have little power over what life sends your way. You can, however, take charge of what you put your focus on, what you allow into your consciousness. Newspapers, magazines, TV, radio, the internet are typically filled with stories of death, destruction, pain, and suffering. Or, perhaps, the tribulations of the celebrity du jour.

If you permit such malevolence and delusion to continuously permeate your mind, it's easy to become overwhelmed with fear, anger, envy, and other negative emotions. You begin to actually believe that the world is a dangerous and heartless place. And if that's what you believe, that's what you'll find.

To be happy, consciously choose what you'll allow into your mind. Spend time reading books and magazines that encourage and inspire you. Watch movies and TV shows that are uplifting and funny. To jump-start the process, consider a media fast during which you eliminate all electronic and print media for a given amount of time to create space for greater happiness and joy.

We should consider every day lost on which we have not danced at least once. And we should call every truth false which was not accompanied by at least one laugh.

~Friedrich Nietzsche

Take time to play

We adults are supposed to take ourselves and life very seriously, right? Wrong! We need time to play and have fun just like kids do.

Many of us have forgotten how to be silly, to act goofy, to just let go and let our childlike impulses take over. So turn off the inner critic that demands, "Act your age." Cut loose and skip, laugh, dance, sing, giggle, play games, have a pillow fight, throw caution to the wind.

To be happier, how about setting up a play date for yourself and some friends today?

People spend a lifetime searching for happiness, looking for peace. They chase idle dreams, addictions, religions, even other people, hoping to fill the emptiness that plagues them. The irony is the only place they ever needed tosearch was within.

~Ramona L. Anderson

Handle your addictions

An addiction can be defined as an unrelenting compulsion by an individual to engage in a particular activity, usually to their detriment.

An incomplete list of possible addictions includes sex, shopping, gambling, web surfing, sleeping, people pleasing, perfectionism, overachieving, hyper-religiosity, pornography, overeating, overworking, and drugs (including alcohol and tobacco).

To move toward greater happiness, acknowledge your addiction(s) and handle them in a way that works for you. You may wish to seek professional help, the support of a 12-step group, or go cold turkey. And remember, there's no time like the present.

We are not human beings having a spiritual experience. We are spiritual beings having a human experience.

~Teilhard de Chardin

Engage in a spiritual practice

What feeds your inner self? What awakens your spirit? What opens your heart? Is it an inspirational observance at your house of faith? An intimate conversation with a cherished friend? A long walk in the forest? An early morning meditation?

Whatever provides you with inner nourishment, whatever feeds that deepest part of yourself, set aside a regular period of time for it, and make it a top priority. Your happiness depends on it.

A happy life must be to a great extent a quiet life, for it is only in an atmosphere of quiet that true joy dare live.

~Bertrand Russell

Take time for solitude

In many societies time alone has become rare. But occasionally you need to spend some time by yourself to recharge your batteries, to nurture yourself, to discern next steps, to remember who you really are.

Occasional solitude is especially essential for partners in a committed relationship. It provides some space in the togetherness. It reminds us that we are quite capable of functioning on our own. It shows us that we are not joined at the hip. It gives us room to do exactly what we want when we want to do it. And it opens the space for us to remember why we love our partner as we do.

For your happiness and for that of those around you, take some time today for solitude.

Successful people turn everyone who can help them into sometime mentors!

~John Crosby

Find a mentor

A mentor is sometimes described as someone whose hindsight can become your foresight. Each of us can benefit from a mentor who is farther down the path of life than we are.

If you want to be a writer, find a writer who will help guide you in your efforts. If you want to be a golfer, shoot a few holes with someone who plays the game better than you and is willing to offer you tips. If you want to succeed in business, align yourself with a businessperson who has been successful, and find out how he or she did it. If you want to be a nurturing parent, look around for a mother or father who has successfully raised children and ask that person to share what he or she knows.

There is no need to figure it all out on your own. Gain the support of a trusted mentor, and notice how your happiness grows.

HAPPINESS AND AUTHENTICITY

*Your results, in fact,
are your true intentions.*

~Brad Brown

Keep reminding yourself that you are it. No one else is responsible for your happiness, fulfillment, satisfaction, competence, health, or life situation but you.

~Kevin Cashman

Become fully accountable

To determine what you want, look at what you've got. That might not be easy to hear, but consciously or unconsciously, you have created your present life just as it is, just as you wanted it.

You might say, but I don't want this debt, divorce, et cetera. And yet at some level, you do. For if you'd truly wanted something different, you would have created that instead.

When you take full responsibility for your life, there's no one to blame. You are empowered to consciously create the life you've been dreaming of and generate more happiness in your life.

Want to really be happy? In every sticky situation ask yourself, "How did I help to create this, and what can I do to resolve it?" In doing so, you become the master of your domain and the architect of your reality.

For peace of mind, resign as general manager of the universe.

~Larry Eisenberg

Resign as emperor of the universe

Do you believe that you know how things should be? How others should be? How life should be?

Well, guess again. You merely create anxiety and suffering for yourself when you act as though you know what's right and what's wrong, what's good and what's bad, what's appropriate and what's not. And you create separation from those around you when you try to force your views on them.

Though many of us believe that we know how life should be, this viewpoint is fallacious and ill-advised. As one sage said, you can be right or you can be happy. Which do you choose?

Happiness begins with our choice to say "yes" to whatever Life gave us, whether we wanted it or not.

~Brad Brown

Notice the messages life sends

Many of us are sleepwalking through life, and we aren't even aware of it. We have been indoctrinated by our parents, relatives, friends, teachers, preachers, politicians, and others to take on beliefs that are theirs—and not necessarily universal truths.

We generally remain in our trance-like state until life sends us a wake-up call. Even then, like the drunk who's in denial, we may refuse to come to grips with reality. Like the pretense of a loveless marriage, we may be unwilling to confront the truth. But if we don't acknowledge the gift in even the most horrific event, discern its meaning for us, and correct the course we are on, one thing is certain: When life wants to get our attention again, the next wake-up call will be even bigger than the one that came before it.

To create greater personal happiness, pay attention to what life brings your way today, determine the message that's there for you, and purposely choose your response.

The summit of happiness is reached when a person is ready to be what he is.

~Desiderius Erasmus

Live authentically

We all want to love and be loved, so it's understandable that in our youth we responded to the desires of parents and others who expected us to grow up to be doctors and lawyers and such. It's understandable that we stuffed our anger or held back our tears. It's understandable that we took on their religion/moral code/politics/worldview.

But by doing so, our authenticity, our spirit, our passion for life, our happiness receded, and we became shadows of our former selves, unaware of who we truly are.

If we are to be happy, we must each wake up and regain our authenticity by peeling back the layers beneath which we've hidden our true selves. Few are willing to risk this journey without significant motivation. We've been deceiving ourselves for so long, it seems that this is just the way life is. Yet in this moment, you have an opportunity to begin living with greater awareness, enthusiasm, and happiness. Will you begin?

Value-based happiness is a sense that our lives have meaning and fulfill some larger purpose. It represents a spiritual source of satisfaction, stemming from our deeper purpose and values.

~Steven Reiss

Live your deepest values

A value is a principle, standard, or quality that is considered desirable or valuable. Courage, compassion, loyalty, generosity, honesty, and humility are just a few examples.

What are your deepest values? Not the values you think you "should" have; the ones that are dearest to you, the ones that help define who you truly are.

Make a list of your top five values. Are you actually living these values? If you're not sure, look at your checkbook stubs and see where you're putting your money. Look at your schedule for the past few weeks and see where you're putting your time.

If you find you are living your values, how does this affect your happiness? And if you're not, what will you do to change this?

Happiness is when what you think, what you say, and what you do are in harmony.

~Mahatma Gandhi

Reclaim your integrity

According to some, integrity is doing the right thing, even when nobody will ever know it. Behaviors of a person with integrity might include honesty, sincerity, truthfulness, steadfastness, accountability, punctuality, ethics, and justice.

Many people talk a good game. But individuals with true integrity take actions that match their words and declarations. For example, if someone professes to believe in justice for all, then it must follow that even the pariahs of society should be given an even break in our legal system.

Living with integrity fosters self-respect and self-esteem, both of which are essential for happiness. Conversely, someone who is "out of integrity" diminishes his self-respect and self-esteem, leading, obviously, to unhappiness. Remember too that there are no minor lapses in integrity. You are either in, or you're out.

Where are you out of integrity right now? What will you do to handle it? When will you do it?

As soon as you honor the present moment, all unhappiness and struggle dissolve, and life begins to flow with joy and ease.

~Eckhart Tolle

Live in the moment

Are you habitually ensnared in the past? Do you frequently find yourself jumping ahead to the future? Or are you generally present in the moment?

If you're like most of us, you create much of your unhappiness by your inability to live in the here and now. You spend up to 90 percent of your time thinking about past disappointments or worrying about some event in a future that hasn't yet arrived.

Take your happiness into your hands by focusing on being fully present in the moment. When your mind starts backtracking to a past event, bring your attention back to right now. When your mind wants to start making up scary stories about something that might take place in the future, bring your attention back to right here, right now.

*The mind is its own place, and in itself,
can make heaven of Hell,
and a hell of Heaven.*

~John Milton

Tame your inner critic

Beneath your conscious level of thinking, your inner critic automatically, harshly, and incessantly passes judgment on everything—from you, to those around you, even to life itself.

Out of these judgments arise separating emotions (anxiety, fear, sadness, depression, hate). You feel lethargic and apathetic. You become emotionally disconnected from the people in your life. Your enthusiasm wanes. Your creativity is inhibited. You lose touch with the best part of yourself.

To become happier, tame your inner critic by taking the following steps:

1. Notice when separating emotions arise.
2. Quietly listen to the voice of your inner critic.
3. Determine whether the critic's statements are true or false (Nine out of ten are false.).
4. For every false statement, respond with what is true for you.
5. Choose how you will be and what you will do going forward.
6. Do it now!

You can't just change how you think or the way that you act. . . . You must gain control over the patterns that govern your mind: your worldview, your beliefs about what you deserve and what's possible.

~Peter Koestenbaum

Dispose of limiting beliefs

Some of us think that our beliefs are a permanent part of who we are. The truth is that our beliefs are learned through our early interactions with our parents, siblings, teachers, preachers, peers, and others. Some of these beliefs probably serve you, while others hold you back.

So the bad news is that you have taken on limiting beliefs about yourself, others, and the world. But the good news is that, regardless of how long you've held these fallacious judgments, you can unlearn them. And you can live out of the truth of who you really are.

Don't trust those who tell you change is impossible. That's just another limiting belief and an excuse for staying where you are. If you like the life you've created, great. But if you are not fully satisfied, if you want to be happier, find a counselor, a personal development program, or another resource, and take action to begin changing your beliefs now.

When you realize you've made a mistake, make amends immediately. It's easier to eat crow while it's still warm.

~Dan Heist

Handle disconnections as you go

To really be happy, handle upsets, misunderstandings, and disagreements as they occur. When you find yourself frustrated, irritated, or annoyed, acknowledge what you're feeling. Don't push your emotions away. Pause, take a few deep breaths, then take appropriate action.

If it's a minor misunderstanding, sometimes a sincere "sorry about that" is sufficient. However, a disrespectful or unloving action that has created an emotional disconnection with another may require a heartfelt apology for your actions and even a request for forgiveness.

Remember that whatever the current situation is, you have had a role in creating it. Thus, you have the power to create something different, including greater connection and happiness, whenever you choose.

Step 8. Made a list of all persons we had harmed and became willing to make amends to them all.

~Alcoholics Anonymous

Bless your past and let it go

Each of us has unfinished business from our past. This excess baggage keeps us hooked to a bygone era of our lives and prevents us from living fully in the present.

To really be happy, it is essential that we handle our past. So without being hard on yourself while doing so, make a list of everything in your past you want to deal with. Then make plans to:

- Finish projects or officially conclude them.
- Collect money that is owed you, and pay all debts you owe.
- Get closure with former spouses and lovers.
- Make amends with those toward whom you've acted unlovingly or disrespectfully.
- Handle anything else about which you feel regret, guilt, or shame.

Though this project may take a while, the effort is worth it. Without this drain on your energy, you will find more mental and emotional space for greater happiness in your life.

If you put yourself in a position where you have to stretch outside your comfort zone, then you are forced to expand your consciousness.

~Les Brown

Stretch yourself regularly

Many of us go through life believing that there is a ceiling beyond which we dare not venture. Thus, it's important to stretch ourselves beyond our self-imposed limitations.

You might believe that you can run only a mile or two at a slow pace. But what if you joined a running group and six months later found yourself finishing a marathon? You might believe you're trapped in a dead-end job. But what if you got more education, then found a position that really suited you? You might believe that letting the real you come out isn't safe. But what if you went on a retreat that evoked you to be your authentic self?

When you go beyond your perceived limits in one area of your life, you realize that it's possible in other areas as well. When you have completed something you weren't sure you could do, you feel more self-assured, more enthusiastic, more inspired, and happier. Possibilities expand, you expand, your life expands, your happiness expands!

The ritual moments of life mark changes from moment to moment, day to day, year to year, and from one stage to another. The conscious acknowledgements of the changes are called rites of passage.

~Robert Fulghum

Create meaningful rituals

Rituals are symbolic acts intended to transform what is often ordinary in your life into the sacred. For example, you might make journaling about your dreams each morning a daily ritual. Or you could start a gratitude ritual at your evening meal. Visiting the elderly members of your family during the holidays could become an annual ritual. You could also read to your child each night at bedtime. You could create an altar where you keep sacred objects and pictures of those who are in need of healing energy or prayer.

Recognize the blessings in the everyday by creating and observing meaningful rituals in your life, then see how your happiness grows.

*Whatever is worth doing at all
is worth doing well.*

~Lord Chesterfield

Do your best in all you do

Doing your best does not mean doing something perfectly. Nor does it mean that you must suffer for your art/job/athletic endeavor/et cetera. It means doing the best you can do in that moment in time, taking into account your current physical and mental state and the level of resources at your disposal.

Most of us endeavor to do our best in order to obtain a reward of some sort—praise from our friends, a year-end bonus from our boss, a loving gesture from our romantic partner. However, the real reason for doing your best is the satisfaction you gain from doing so.

When you are intent on doing your best, you become engrossed in what you are doing, you are in the flow, you are filled with energy, you perform without effort. And even if no one else acknowledges you, you gain a profound sense of contentment and happiness.

Twenty years from now you will be more disappointed by the things you didn't do than the ones you did do. So throw off the bowlines. Sail away from the safe harbor. Catch the trade winds in your sails.

~Mark Twain

Dwell in a locale that fits

Frequently we find ourselves living in a geographical region because of family, employment opportunities, love interests, the fear of change, or just plain old inertia. What if you made a conscious choice about where you live?

Make a list of the qualities you want in your ideal location—city or rural; large population or small; mountains, coastal, or inland; et cetera. Then prioritize that list. Now determine some locations where those qualities can be found. Which of these seem to be perfect for you?

Be bold. Talk to folks who live (or have lived) in some of the places that appear to have the qualities you want. Research some of them. Visit several of the locales to find out what they're really like. Then consider making a move.

How would your happiness level change if you were living in a place that's ideal for you?

HAPPINESS IN RELATIONSHIPS

There is only one happiness in life, to love and be loved.

~George Sand

You, yourself, as much as anybody in the entire universe, deserve your love and affection.

~Buddha

Love and nurture yourself

Many of us spend so much time focusing on our relationships with others, we tend to neglect our relationship with ourselves. However, we are not available to really love others or be loved by them until we've learned to love and nurture ourselves.

Here are a few tips to help you nurture your relationship with yourself and become happier in the process.

- When the voice of your inner critic creeps in, turn it off and put your focus elsewhere.
- Affirm who you really are daily by looking in a mirror and stating the things you like about yourself.
- Take a bubble bath with your favorite music in the background and candles all around.
- Forgive yourself for any real or imagined transgressions from your past.

Nurturing yourself finally comes down to a choice. What will you choose?

A friend is someone who knows the song in your heart and can sing it back to you when you have forgotten the words.

~Unknown

Surround yourself with supporters

What sort of people have you attracted into your life? Do they "get" who you are and what you're about in the world? Or do they seem to think you should live up to their expectations? Do you feel connected to them in a deep way? Or is there frequent disconnection because they consistently do or say things that are judgmental, unloving, or disrespectful? When you're around them, do you feel energized? Or do you feel drained of energy? Are they "there" for you during challenging times? Or are they content to merely offer advice and solutions based on their perspectives and beliefs?

Perhaps it's time to let go of relationships that don't serve you. Perhaps it's time to surround yourself with people who nurture you, who understand and respect your hopes and dreams, who support you to walk your talk, who hold you when you hurt.

Surround yourself with people who genuinely love you, and feel your happiness grow.

When you are for me as much as you are for yourself, and I am for you as much as I am for myself, we will start to understand the meaning of our relationship.

~Brad Brown

Create a loving relationship

The process of creating a conscious relationship is a sacred journey, an evolving partnership in which both partners are fully committed to loving, honoring, and respecting one another and themselves. Below are some practices for creating such a relationship.

- Choose to fully commit—all the way.
- Create vows or commitments that you intend to follow throughout your time together.
- Tell the truth even when you believe it might be challenging for the other to hear.
- Focus on what is working in the relationship and the positive attributes of one another.
- Let go of ill will and practice forgiveness.
- Support one another to be fully authentic.

How do you think your happiness level would rise if you followed these practices?

Present your family and friends with their eulogies now—they won't be able to hear how much you love them and appreciate them from inside the coffin.

~Anonymous

Deepen all your relationships

We all want to love and be loved. Our happiness grows in direct proportion to our ability to give and receive love. Yet we sometimes have a challenging time doing so.

If you want to create stronger connections to those who are important to you, accept and love them just as they are. Refrain from criticizing them. Be heartfelt and frequent in your acknowledgments, and forgive them for any real or perceived transgressions. Be available to hear their fears and frustrations without getting drawn in. Finally, be open about your desires, and encourage them to do the same.

Will you do what's necessary to deepen your relationships? You're bound to become a lot happier when you do.

Your children are not your children, they are the sons and daughters of life's longing for itself. They come through you, but not from you. And though they are with you, they do not belong to you.

~Khalil Gibran

Treat your children well

When Reverend Howard Hanger baptizes a baby, his charge to the parents is the highlight of the ritual for me: "Will you raise this child to be the person God meant her to be, not the person you think she should be? If you will, say 'I will.'"

Many of us have unfulfilled dreams and visions; if we aren't conscious of these aspirations, we may pass them on to our kids in the vain hope that they might live out our forsaken dreams for us. On the other hand, we may just want what we consider best for our child. Yet what we consider best might not be.

Each child who enters the world is unique, each with his or her own special gift. Our job is to love and respect our children unconditionally just as they are, open the door to as many opportunities for growth and awareness as possible, then let them spread their wings and fly. We don't have to tell them what to do or how to be; they already know much better than we.

*Really hug the person you are hugging.
Make him/her very real in your arms.
Breathe consciously and hug him/her with
all your body, spirit and heart.*

~Thich Nhat Hanh

More hugs = more happiness

We humans are social beings hardwired to respond to the loving touch of another. In fact, scientific studies have shown that human touch lowers the output of cortisol, a stress hormone, and causes an increase in two "happiness-inducing" brain chemicals—serotonin and dopamine.

Hugs are one way we connect with loved ones. Some of us hug with openness and enthusiasm. Some of us hug more cautiously. And some of us settle for the more formal handshake.

There's no right way or wrong way to hug; the main thing is to do your best to really connect with the person you're hugging. A few suggestions from the Hugs for Health Foundation:

- Always respect another's space and ask permission before hugging.
- Remember that a hug is a compassionate, gentle gesture.
- Endeavor to be fully present when hugging.

I believe life is constantly testing us for our level of commitment, and life's greatest rewards are reserved for those who demonstrate a never-ending commitment to act until they achieve. This level of resolve can move mountains, but it must be constant and consistent.

~Anthony Robbins

Fully commit

Your level of commitment—to a job, a cause, or a relationship—is the result of a choice you have made, either consciously or unconsciously.

In a given situation, your level of commitment is likely not a constant; you might move from uncommitted, to obligated, to committed, and back again over a period of time. But when you're in all the way, the space is opened for others to join you. And when that happens, there's no more looking around for something better, no more "should I stay or should I go," no more exit strategies. You're on solid ground and can relax and enjoy life.

Are you fully committed to your relationship? To your job? To the organization you volunteer with? If you chose to fully commit, how do you think your happiness level would grow?

The first duty of love is to listen.
~Paul Tillich

Hear and be heard

To be happy, it's essential to truly hear and be heard. But often when we're engaged in conversation and someone else is talking, we're more interested in what we're going to say next, defending ourselves, or considering what's for dinner.

If you really want to listen you must make a conscious effort to understand the other person's point of view. More than simply hearing the words being spoken, you must also listen with your eyes, heart, and gut. A few tips for doing so:

- Enter into the conversation with an intention to hear and understand the other person.
- Help him/her feel safe enough to communicate fully and honestly with you.
- Listen to the other person's words with compassion and do your best to grasp what she/he is saying.
- Express your compassion and openness nonverbally, and maintain eye contact without staring.
- Allow the other person to speak without interruption until he or she is finished. Then reflect back what has been said.

Keep on asking, and you will be given what you ask for. Keep on looking, and you will find. Keep on knocking, and the door will be opened. For everyone who asks, receives. Everyone who seeks, finds. And the door is opened to everyone who knocks.

~Matthew 7:7-8

Ask for what you want

Want to be happy? Ask for what you want. For example, you might let your significant other know what words you find affirming, how you like to be physically touched, or how you want to be comforted when you're feeling low. By doing so, you can also open the space for your partner to share his or her desires with you.

Asking for what you want doesn't guarantee you'll get it, so don't set up expectations in this regard. However, asking increases the odds that you will. Plus it eliminates the need for others in your life to make dubious assumptions, take uniformed guesses, or try to read your mind. When you make your desires clear, while making no demands, those around you have the opportunity to respond accordingly.

A "No" uttered from deepest conviction is better and greater than a "Yes" merely uttered to please, or what is worse, to avoid trouble.

~Mahatma Gandhi

Clearly state "yes" or "no"

When someone makes a request of you, respond with a clear yes or a clear no. You'll make your life simpler and happier if you'll follow this basic principle.

If the request is something you absolutely want to do, you'll know it in that moment. In this instance, just give an enthusiastic yes. If, on the other hand, you know you don't want to do it, don't hesitate. Just give a firm but compassionate no.

You might need to check your calendar or get further information. However, "I'll try to" or "I'll think about it" or "Maybe" are typically just ways to waffle and keep yourself and the requestor in limbo.

Create greater happiness for yourself by clearly stating yes or no.

*No one can hurt you
without your consent.*

~Eleanor Roosevelt

Don't take it personally

When someone says something unloving or disrespectful to you, it's essential to remember that the statement is really about him or her, not you. When you do so, you eliminate unnecessary suffering and keep your happiness at a higher level.

Suppose a friend says, "You're the most selfish person I know." You can take this statement personally, feel hurt, and start describing all the generous things you've done recently. Or you can realize that this is your friend's own self-judgment projected onto you and refuse to take the criticism to heart.

It's important to remember that we're not always at our best and to allow for times when a friend or relative is having a bad day. Nonetheless, if someone in your life does or says unloving and disrespectful things frequently, it's probably time to consider whether that relationship really serves you or your happiness.

The purpose of having boundaries is to protect and take care of ourselves.

~Robert Burney

Establish boundaries

You train people to treat you exactly the way you want to be treated. Is this good news? Are your friends loving, respectful, and supportive of you? Or do they make critical comments, act inappropriately, or explain how they think you should be living your life?

Stand up for yourself by setting boundaries Here are a few samples to get you started:

- I will only be with people who are straightforward and honest with me.
- I will only be in relationship with people who really listen to me and honor what I'm saying.
- I will not tolerate anyone yelling at me or dumping their anger on me.
- I will give my friends and associates the space to be human and make mistakes, but I will free myself from toxic relationships.

Yes, you can have boundaries and still have friends. True friends will honor what you're going for and get onboard. Some may not and may leave. Either way, when you set and maintain boundaries, your happiness level will rise.

Basically, the only thing we need is a hand that rests on our own, that wishes it well, that sometimes guides us.

~Hector Bianciotti

Create a support network

To really be happy it's important to have a network of supportive friends and family members. You are there to provide your support when asked; likewise, they are there for you. Here are a few guidelines for offering support:

- Be fully present, attentive, patient, and compassionate.
- Ask what support is wanted.
- Listen quietly without judgment.
- Acknowledge them for where they are and their willingness to be vulnerable.
- Offer occasional questions to gain greater clarity and to deepen sharing.
- Provide your opinion only if its asked for.
- Empathize, but don't take on their emotions.
- When asked to do so, tell your truth with compassion.
- Avoid trying to fix it.

A network of truly supportive friends may take a while to build, but you'll be happier knowing they're there.

HAPPINESS . . . TO JOY

You are powerful. Whatever you set your mind on having, you will have. Whatever you decide to be, you will be. The evidence is all around you. The power of your will has brought you precisely to where you are right now.

~Ralph Marston

You are never given a dream without also being given the power to make it true. You may have to work for it, however.

~Richard Bach

Create a vision for yourself

What is your vision for your life? What do you want to accomplish, who do you want to be . . . in five years? In ten years? At the end of your time in your physical body?

When you are in touch with a compelling mental picture of an ideal future for yourself, it can support you in the following ways:

- A powerful vision has an excellent chance of becoming reality.
- The choices and actions necessary to make your vision a reality become clearer.
- The energy required flows freely.
- A vision can inspire you to overcome the challenges you confront.
- You are typically drawn inexorably toward the cherished dream.

Find a quiet place, breathe deeply, relax, and take some time to envision your ideal future. When you see yourself several years from now, how do you feel? Inspired? Fulfilled? Peaceful? Happy?

Many persons have a wrong idea of what constitutes true happiness. It is not attained through self-gratification but through fidelity to a worthy purpose.

~Helen Keller

Live your purpose

Your purpose in life is an undeniable element of who you are and why you are here on this planet.

Your purpose may lurk beneath the surface of your consciousness, just waiting to be discovered. And if you are willing to take heed, life will send you synchronicities, dreams, visions, insights, and unexpected opportunities to awaken you to it.

Perhaps you've had some inkling, some vision of what you're called to do. Perhaps you're bored with the work you're doing now and understand that it's time for a change. Perhaps you've become aware of a special talent that's been dormant. Perhaps a serendipitous meeting has awakened you to new possibilities.

Now is the time. Step into your purpose with passion, and feel how your happiness grows!

*We would do well to appreciate . . .
that every thought is sacred, with
the power to take physical form.*

~Lynne McTaggart

Harness the power of intention

Scientific experiments have proven what indigenous cultures have known for centuries—human thought can affect physical matter. Focused intention has helped plants grow faster, injuries heal, and crime rates drop.

So can we really manifest our reality and engender greater happiness? Yes, but it takes conscious thought, speaking and acting in alignment with who we are and what we say we want, then allowing life to bring it forth.

Let's say you want an ideal romantic partner. First you must create and hold a clear vision of this person in your mind's eye. When you speak of what you're going for, you say it in words that express your belief that this person will soon be with you. Then you remain open for life to deliver.

What do you want to manifest? Will you focus your intention to move toward making your desire a reality?

Humankind did not weave the web of life. We are but strands within it. Whatever we do to the web, we do to ourselves.

~Chief Seattle

Appreciate the web of life

We humans have come to think we're superior to the other animals, creating disconnection and unhappiness in the process. We have believed that what we do to other species does not affect us. So we have exploited our planet, frequently at the other species' expense. And now we realize that it has been at our own expense as well.

We must come to grips with the fact that we are energetically connected with other animals and plants. When you understand this, you will help to protect the rain forests, the polar bears, even the spider that just crawled on your leg. For as you nurture them, you nurture yourself.

Take a few moments to consider how you might act differently toward members of the animal and plant kingdoms when you take into account your deep and abiding connection with them.

The place God calls you to is the place where your deep gladness and the world's deep hunger meet.

~Frederick Buechner

Share your gifts through service

To be truly happy, we must discover our unique gifts and share them with the world. Each of us has a gift, at least one—writing, gardening, dancing, organizing—that we can make the most of . . . once we remember what it is.

When we share our gifts, we are serving others. However, in doing so, humility is required. For as Lilla Watson once said, "If you are coming to help me, you are wasting your time. But if you are coming because your liberation is bound up with mine, then let us work together."

Though vitally important, your personal impact on the world may be almost imperceptible. But when many others join together, a noticeable shift occurs. When one person throws his or her stone in the pool, the water level does not appear to rise, even though it has. When millions of us throw our stones in the pool, however, the water overflows its banks in a manner that cannot be denied.

The most certain way to succeed is always to try just one more time.

~Thomas A. Edison

Keep on keeping on

If you want to successfully move toward your vision for yourself, if you want greater happiness in your life, it is essential to persevere, even in the face of challenges or discouragement.

If you can envision what you truly want, you can create it. See yourself having it in your mind's eye. Work toward it on a daily basis. Seek counsel from someone who's already done it. Handle your inner critic and those in your life who plant seeds of doubt. Surround yourself with people who support you. Know that every no you get brings you closer to a yes. Learn from each setback. Change course if necessary. Keep your eye on the ball. And refuse to give up!

HAPPY ENDINGS

As a well-spent day brings happy sleep, so a life well used brings happy death.

~Leonardo da Vinci

Warriors live with death at their side, and from the knowledge that death is with them, they draw the courage to face anything.

~Don Juan

Make friends with death

When you've come to grips with arguably the worst thing that can happen to you, there's nothing holding you back from living your life in a way that truly fits . . . except you.

We're all going to die. To live a happy life means being conscious of this, feeling gratitude for the time we've been given, and being ready to go at any moment—affairs in order, everything said that is to be said, everything done that is to be done, forgiveness extended, loose ends handled.

Take some time now to write your own obituary. Write it in the third person (He was honored by. . . Her favorite trip was . . .). Be sure to include memberships in organizations, causes you took up, your achievements, your favorite recollections, what you want people to remember about you, plus anything else you want to include.

When you read your obituary how do you feel? Is there any action you wish to take as a result of this experience?

If you were going to die soon and had only one phone call you could make, whom would you call and what would you say? And why are you waiting?

~Stephen Levine

Things to do before you die

1. **Make peace with your past.** Take care of all unfinished business.
2. **Acknowledge those who are important to you.** Tell them what they mean to you every chance you get.
3. **Love yourself and others well.** Love is one of the greatest gifts we have to give. Give it gladly.
4. **Give thanks.** Take time to give thanks for the blessings in life and notice how your outlook is brightened.
5. **Make your final arrangements.** Making these decisions now lifts a burden from your loved ones, who will have enough to deal with when you die. By putting you face to face with your mortality, this step can also motivate you to live as you truly want to, instead of how you think you should.
6. **Leave a legacy.** Knowing that you've made a positive impact adds meaning and fulfillment to your life. Remember to acknowledge yourself for your contributions.

Ah, but I was so much older then; I'm younger than that now.

~Bob Dylan

About the author

In an earlier incarnation, Bruce Mulkey was a cynical football-playing, pickup-truck-driving, beer-swilling, misogynistic womanizer who built log houses for a living. Having miraculously survived that era, he now is a politically progressive, spiritually aware, bike-riding, cat-loving writer living happily with his wife, Shonnie Lavender, their daughter, Gracelyn, and their three feline family members, Bandit, Desmond, and Kaali, in the eclectic Southern Appalachian city of Asheville, North Carolina.

Contact information

E-mail: bruce@brucemulkey.com

Bruce Mulkey's Blog: brucemulkey.com